Collins

KS3
Science
Year 7
Workbook

Ian Honeysett, Sam Holyman and Lynn Pharaoh

About this Workbook

There are three Collins workbooks for KS3 Science:
Year 7 Science ISBN 9780008553722
Year 8 Science ISBN 9780008553739
Year 9 Science ISBN 9780008553746

Together they provide topic-based practice for all the skills and content on the Programme of Study for Key Stage 3 Science.

Questions for each topic have been organised into sections that test different **skills**.

- Vocabulary Builder
- Maths Skills
- Testing Understanding
- Working Scientifically
- Science in Use

Found throughout the book, the **QR codes** can be scanned on your smartphone. Each QR code links to a video working through the solution to one of the questions or question parts on the double-page spread.

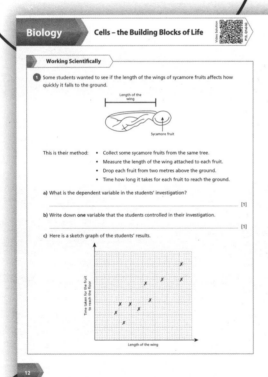

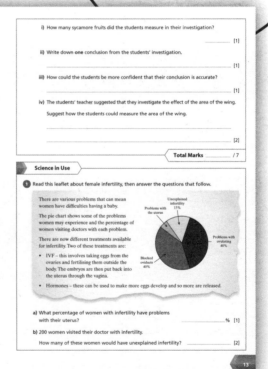

Track your progress by recording your marks in the box at the end of each skills section and the summary box at the end of each topic.

The **answers** are included at the back of the book so that you can mark your own work.

If you get a question wrong, make sure you read the answer carefully so that you understand where you went wrong.

Helpful tips are also included.

Contents

Biology

Chemistry

Physics

Answers

Acknowledgements

The authors and publisher are grateful to the copyright holders for permission to use quoted materials and images.

All images are ©Shutterstock.com or © HarperCollins*Publishers*

Every effort has been made to trace copyright holders and obtain their permission for the use of copyright material. The authors and publisher will gladly receive information enabling them to rectify any error or omission in subsequent editions. All facts are correct at time of going to press.

Published by Collins
An imprint of HarperCollins*Publishers*
1 London Bridge Street
London SE1 9GF

HarperCollins*Publishers*
Macken House
39/40 Mayor Street Upper
Dublin 1
D01 C9W8
Ireland

© HarperCollins*Publishers* Limited 2023

ISBN 9780008553722

10 9 8 7 6 5 4 3 2

All rights reserved. No part of this publication may be reproduced, stored in a retrieval system, or transmitted, in any form or by any means, electronic, mechanical, photocopying, recording or otherwise, without the prior permission of Collins.

British Library Cataloguing in Publication Data.

A CIP record of this book is available from the British Library.

Publisher: Clare Souza
Commissioning: Richard Toms
Authors: Ian Honeysett (Biology),
Sam Holyman (Chemistry) and Lynn Pharaoh (Physics)
Project editors: Charlotte Christensen and Katie Galloway
Cover Design: Kevin Robbins and Sarah Duxbury
Inside Concept Design: Sarah Duxbury and Paul Oates
Text Design and Layout: Contentra Technologies
Production: Emma Wood
Printed in India by Multivista Global Pvt. Ltd.

MIX
Paper | Supporting responsible forestry
FSC™ C007454

This book is produced from independently certified FSC™ paper to ensure responsible forest management.

For more information visit:
www.harpercollins.co.uk/green

Biology — Cells – the Building Blocks of Life

Vocabulary Builder

1 a) Draw lines to join each part of the cell with its correct function.

Part of the Cell	Function
Chloroplast	Releases energy from food
Mitochondria	Contains DNA to control the reactions of the cell
Nucleus	Traps sunlight to produce glucose
Vacuole	Provides pressure to keep the cell in shape

[3]

2 Identify the type of cell from its description.

Choose the type of cell from the box below. Each type of cell can be used only once.

bacterium	euglena	nerve cell	paramecium
root hair cell		sperm cell	

a) A plant cell that has a long projection to absorb water
and minerals from the soil. .... [1]

b) A unicellular prokaryote organism that does not have
a nucleus. .... [1]

c) An animal cell that carries the male genetic information
to the egg cell. .... [1]

d) A type of protozoa that is covered in small hairs called cilia. .... [1]

e) A cell that transmits electrical impulses. .... [1]

f) A unicellular alga that swims using a flagellum. .... [1]

3 This question is about the male and female reproductive systems.

For each part, put a tick to show if each of the statements is **true** or **false**.

a) **Ovary**

	True	False
Produces egg cells	☐	☐
Is where the placenta grows	☐	☐

[2]

b) Oviduct

	True	False	
Where the developing baby grows	☐	☐	
Where fertilisation happens	☐	☐	[2]

c) Sperm duct

	True	False	
Carries sperm through the penis	☐	☐	
Produces sperm	☐	☐	[2]

d) Penis

	True	False	
Delivers sperm into the vagina	☐	☐	
Adds a liquid to the sperm to make semen	☐	☐	[2]

Total Marks _____ / 17

Maths Skills

1 The table shows how the length of a human foetus changes during pregnancy.

Stage of pregnancy (weeks)	5	10	15	20	30	40
Length of foetus (mm)	10	30	100	250	400	480

a) Plot the **length of foetus** versus the **stage of pregnancy** on the graph. The first point has been plotted for you. [2]

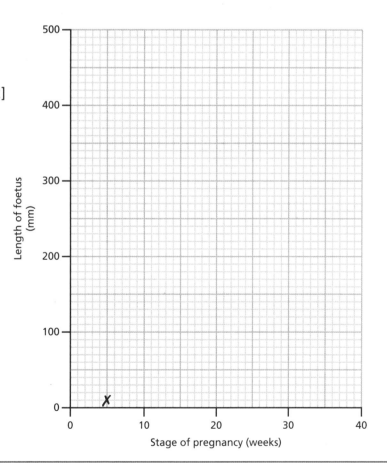

b) Use the points to draw a curve of best fit. [1]

c) Use your graph to estimate the length of the foetus at 25 weeks. .... mm [1]

d) Put a ring around the time when the foetus is growing fastest.

      0 to 5 weeks   **15 to 20 weeks**   **30 to 40 weeks** [1]

e) Write down **one** way that the graph might look different if the mother smoked cigarettes through the pregnancy.

.... [1]

2 The table gives some information about different types of cells and organelles.

Cell / Organelle	Size (mm)
Mitochondria	0.002
Nuclei	0.01
Bacteria	0.002
Cheek cells	0.05
Liver cells	0.05
Plant leaf cells	0.1

a) Which is the smallest organelle shown in the table? .... [1]

b) Which two cells in the table are animal cells?

.... and .... [1]

c) How many times larger are plant leaf cells compared to liver cells?

.... [1]

d) Cells are often measured in micrometres. There are 1000 micrometres to a millimetre.

How large is a nucleus in micrometres? .... micrometres [1]

e) Many scientists think that mitochondria were originally formed from bacteria.
What piece of evidence in the table supports this idea?

.... [1]

Total Marks .... / 11

1 **a)** Complete this diagram showing the levels of organisation in living organisms.

Choose your words from the box. Each word should be used once.

| organisms | organs | system | tissues |

cells ⟶ .... ⟶ .... ⟶ .... ⟶ .... [3]

b) Write down whether each structure is an **organ**, **cell** or **tissue**.

i) Sperm .... [1]

ii) Heart .... [1]

iii) Bone .... [1]

2 The diagram shows seeds or fruits from five different plants.

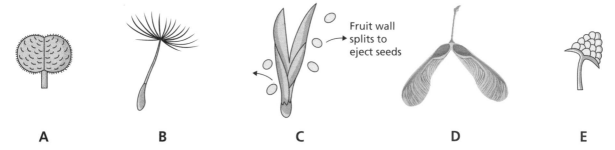

Fruit wall splits to eject seeds

A   B   C   D   E

Complete this table by writing the letters **A–E** in the correct column. (Some columns may have more than one letter and some columns may have no letters.)

Uses wind dispersal	Uses animal dispersal	Uses self-dispersal	Uses water dispersal

[5]

3 Camile wants to use a microscope to look at onion cells.

a) She makes a microscope slide to show stained onion cells.

Here is the apparatus she uses:

- Microscope slide   • Cover slip   • Knife   • Stain

Describe how Camile could use the apparatus to make a stained slide of onion cells.

....

....

.... [4]

b) Explain why Camile stains the cells before looking at them with the microscope.

....

....

.... [2]

c) The photograph shows what Camile can see using the microscope.

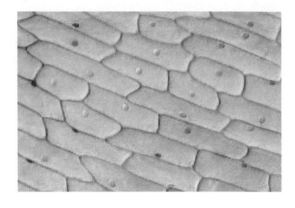

i) In the space below, draw a labelled diagram of **three** of the onion cells from the photograph.

[3]

ii) Write down **two** ways that the cells would be different if they were bacterial cells.

1. ....

2. .... [2]

4 The diagram shows an insect-pollinated flower with parts labelled A–H.

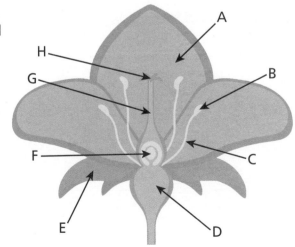

a) Use the letters from the diagram to complete this table.

Structure	Letter
Petal	
Ovule	
Anther	
Stigma	

[4]

b) Which two letters show where pollen is transferred during pollination?

from .... to .... [2]

c) Which letter shows the structure that becomes a seed? .... [1]

d) Wind-pollinated flowers have a different structure to insect-pollinated flowers. Complete these sentences to show these differences.

Wind-pollinated flowers need to produce more pollen and so they have larger

.... To catch the pollen, they have feathery ....

that hang outside the flower. Wind-pollinated flowers are not brightly coloured and

lack .... as they do not need to attract insects. [3]

5 The diagram shows the male reproductive system.

a) Which of the labelled structures produces sperm?

.... [1]

b) What is the function of the urethra in reproduction?

....

.... [1]

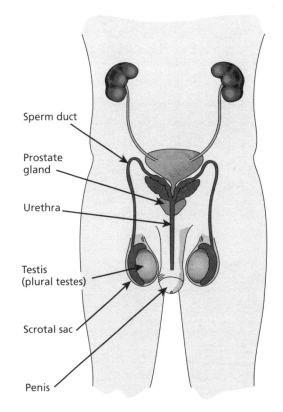

Sperm duct

Prostate gland

Urethra

Testis (plural testes)

Scrotal sac

Penis

c) Some men who do not want to have any (more) children have an operation that cuts the sperm duct.

Explain how this would stop them having any (more) children.

....

....

.... **[2]**

d) The graph shows the number of sperm made on 13 different days.

i) On which day were most sperm made? .... **[1]**

ii) Between day 3 and day 4 the weather becomes much warmer.

Put a tick in the box that describes the decrease in the number of sperm made between day 3 and day 4.

0.3 thousand million ☐   0.6 thousand million ☐

0.9 thousand million ☐   1.2 thousand million ☐ **[1]**

iii) Body temperature is normally higher than the external temperature.

Explain why having the testis in the scrotum is important for sperm production.

....

....

.... **[3]**

6 The diagram shows a foetus growing inside the uterus.

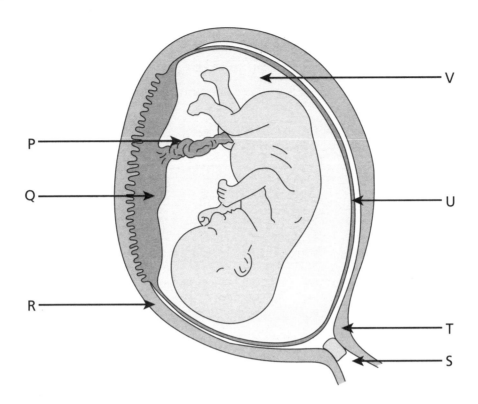

a) Give the letter that labels each of these structures.

   i) The umbilical cord. .... [1]

   ii) The structure that contracts during birth to force
       the baby through the cervix. .... [1]

b) Describe the function of each of these structures:

   i) Structure Q

   ....

   ....

   .... [3]

   ii) Structure V

   ....

   .... [2]

1 Some students wanted to see if the length of the wings of sycamore fruits affects how quickly it falls to the ground.

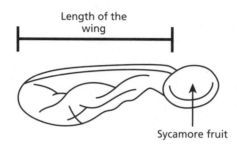

Length of the wing

Sycamore fruit

This is their method:
- Collect some sycamore fruits from the same tree.
- Measure the length of the wing attached to each fruit.
- Drop each fruit from two metres above the ground.
- Time how long it takes for each fruit to reach the ground.

a) What is the dependent variable in the students' investigation?

.... [1]

b) Write down **one** variable that the students controlled in their investigation.

.... [1]

c) Here is a sketch graph of the students' results.

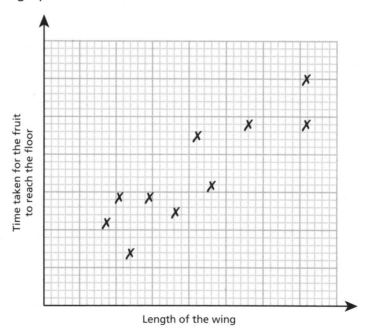

Time taken for the fruit to reach the floor

Length of the wing

i) How many sycamore fruits did the students measure in their investigation?

.... [1]

ii) Write down **one** conclusion from the students' investigation.

.... [1]

iii) How could the students be more confident that their conclusion is accurate?

.... [1]

iv) The students' teacher suggested that they investigate the effect of the area of the wing.

Suggest how the students could measure the area of the wing.

....

.... [2]

Total Marks .... / 7

Science in Use

1 Read this leaflet about female infertility, then answer the questions that follow.

There are various problems that can mean women have difficulties having a baby.

The pie chart shows some of the problems women may experience and the percentage of women visiting doctors with each problem.

There are now different treatments available for infertility. Two of these treatments are:

- IVF – this involves taking eggs from the ovaries and fertilising them outside the body. The embryos are then put back into the uterus through the vagina.

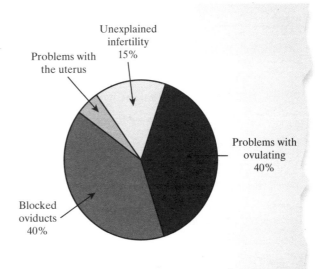

- Hormones – these can be used to make more eggs develop and so more are released.

a) What percentage of women with infertility have problems with their uterus? .... % [1]

b) 200 women visited their doctor with infertility.

How many of these women would have unexplained infertility? .... [2]

13

c) IVF was first used in 1979 to treat infertility.

    i) Which of the female fertility problems listed below is most likely to be treated with IVF?

       Tick **one** box.

       blocked oviducts   ☐

       problems with ovulating   ☐

       problems with the uterus   ☐   [1]

    ii) Explain your answer to part **i)**.

       _____

       _____

       _____ [2]

2 Read this passage about climate change and seed dispersal, then answer the questions that follow.

Is climate change preventing seed dispersal?

Plants use many methods for spreading their seeds away from the parent plant, but more than half of all plants rely on animals to spread their seeds. However, in tropical rainforests, animals spread the seeds of up to 90 per cent of tree species.

Today the Earth is losing species and this might affect seed dispersal. This is particularly the case if we lose birds and mammals that disperse plants. Also, the movement of animals that disperse seeds can be reduced by roads or built-up areas.

Now scientists are studying how problems with seed dispersal can affect how plants respond to climate change.

If climates change, it is important for plants to be able to spread their seeds to new areas. Otherwise, they could be stuck in areas where they will struggle to survive.

There are ways to increase seed dispersal. People can make sure there are wildlife corridors. These are connections between different areas that animals can move along. Protecting important seed dispersers, such as bears, elephants and toucans will also help.

a) Animals, such as bears, are responsible for spreading the seeds of many plants.

Describe **two** ways that they might do this.

1. ....

.... [1]

2. ....

.... [1]

b) If climates change, it is important that plants can spread their seeds to new areas.

Explain why this is important.

....

....

.... [2]

c) Explain why the grass verges that run along the side of motorways are called 'wildlife corridors'.

....

....

.... [2]

Total Marks .... / 12

	Vocabulary Builder	Maths Skills	Testing Understanding	Working Scientifically	Science in Use
Total Marks	.... / 17	.... / 11	.... / 48	.... / 7	.... / 12

Biology — Eating, Drinking and Breathing

Vocabulary Builder

1 Identify these structures in the breathing systems of humans from the descriptions.

Choose the structures from the list in the box.

alveoli	bronchi	bronchioles	diaphragm	ribs	trachea

a) The tube that brings air into the body.

.... [1]

b) A sheet of muscle that contracts when we breathe in.

.... [1]

c) The site of gas exchange.

.... [1]

d) Small tubes that end at the alveoli.

.... [1]

2 Draw lines to join each **disease** to the correct **cause**.

Disease	Cause
anaemia	lack of vitamin C
asthma	lack of iron
lung cancer	tightening of muscles in the bronchioles
rickets	chemicals in cigarette smoke
scurvy	lack of vitamin D

[4]

3 This question is about food and digestion.

For each statement put a tick to show if the statement is **true** or **false**.

a) **Benedict's solution**

	True	False
Is blue in colour	☐	☐
Is used to test for sugars	☐	☐
Turns blue–black in a positive test	☐	☐	[3]

b) **Amylase**

	True	False
Is an enzyme	☐	☐
Digests protein	☐	☐
Is produced in the stomach	☐	☐	[3]

c) **Small intestine**

	True	False
Passes food into the stomach	☐	☐
Makes acid	☐	☐
Absorbs digested food into the blood	☐	☐	[3]

Total Marks .... / 17

Maths Skills

1 The table shows the percentage of different foods in the diets of two children living in two different countries, **A** and **B**.

Food	Percentage of the diet	
	In country A	In country B
Cereals	70	20
Fruit and vegetables	20	35
Meat, fish and eggs	5	25
Others	5	....

a) Calculate the missing percentage in the table. [1]

b) Complete this pie chart by shading in different colours to show the diet for the child living in country **A**.

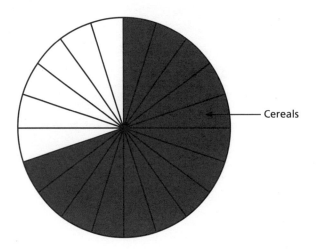

Cereals

[3]

c) i) Calculate how many times greater the meat, fish and eggs percentage is for the child in country **B** compared with the child in country **A**.

_____

_____ [2]

ii) Explain what effect this difference might have on the growth of the two children.

_____

_____

_____ [2]

Total Marks _____ / 8

Testing Understanding

1 The table shows the recommended daily amounts in the diet for three different food nutrients.

They are shown for a 10-year-old girl and a 25-year-old woman.

The amounts have been calculated per kilogram of the person's mass.

	Protein (g)	Iron (mg)	Calcium (mg)
10-year-old	0.5	0.12	9
25-year-old	0.35	0.13	6

a) i) How much more protein does the 10-year-old need per day compared to the 25-year-old?

.... [1]

ii) Give a reason for the difference in the protein needed by the two females.

....

.... [2]

iii) Describe how you could test for protein in a food.

....

.... [2]

b) The 10-year-old girl has not reached puberty.

Explain why she needs less iron than the 25-year-old woman.

....

.... [2]

c) Name a food that is a good source of iron.

.... [1]

2 A teacher sets up a model to demonstrate breathing. They use a glass jar that has no bottom.

They stretch a rubber sheet over the bottom and connect two balloons as shown in the diagram.

a) Write which parts of the model represent the following:

i) The diaphragm .... [1]

ii) The lungs .... [1]

iii) The trachea .... [1]

b) What would happen if the teacher pulled down on the rubber sheet?

Explain your answer.

....

....

.... [3]

3 The diagram shows the human digestive system.

C

A

D

B

E

a) Which letter labels the stomach?

.... [1]

b) Which structure is labelled A?

.... [1]

c) Which letter labels the part of the digestive system that contains most bacteria?

.... [1]

d) How is food moved along structure C?

....

.... [2]

e) What is the role of structure E in making faeces?

....

.... [2]

4 Hassan records his breathing using a machine that makes a trace. He did this while he was resting and straight after exercise.

The trace shows the volume of air he exchanges in each breath and the number of breaths in 30 seconds.

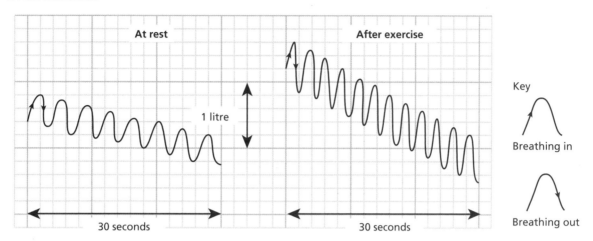

Use the trace to fill in the gaps in these sentences.

At rest Hassan breathes 8 times in 30 seconds.

After exercise he breathes .... times in 30 seconds. This is a breathing

rate of .... breaths per minute.

When resting, each breath exchanged about 0.5 litres of air. After exercise this increased to

about .... litres per breath.

The increase in breathing rate and size of each breath allows Hassan to remove the extra

.... gas that has been produced during exercise. [4]

5 The diagram shows one alveolus (air sac) and a blood vessel in the lungs.

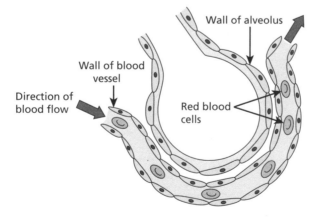

a) Draw **two** labelled arrows to show the direction of movement of these gases between the air and the blood:

   i) Oxygen [1]

   ii) Carbon dioxide [1]

b) Complete these sentences about the movement of these gases.

Oxygen is exchanged between the air and the blood by a process called

.... This process needs a .... gradient

to happen. This gradient is maintained as oxygen is used in the body for

....   [3]

c) Describe how the structures shown in the diagram are adapted to speed up exchange of gases.

In your answer write about:

- surface area
- thickness of the walls
- the distance between the air and the blood.

....

....

....

....   [3]

6 The graph shows the results of a study on two people.

One person was a heavy smoker and the other was a non-smoker.

The study measured the efficiency of the two lungs of the two people.

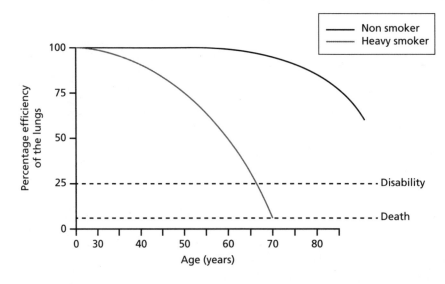

a) Below what percentage efficiency of the lungs does a person become disabled?

_____ % [1]

b) At what age did the heavy smoker die? _____ [1]

c) Describe the effects that heavy smoking has on the lungs.

_____

_____

_____

_____ [3]

d) Why would it be difficult to draw any conclusions about the effects of smoking from just this study?

_____

_____ [2]

Total Marks _____ / 40

Working Scientifically

1 A student wants to compare the amount of energy in different foods. They decide to set the food alight and use the burning food to heat water.

This is the method they use for each food:

1. Put 20 cm³ of water into a boiling tube.
2. Measure the temperature of the water.
3. Put the food sample on a mounted needle.
4. Set fire to the food and hold it under the boiling tube.
5. Measure the temperature of the water when the food is fully burned.

Here is a diagram of their experimental set up.

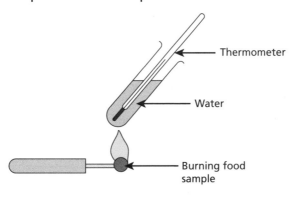

Thermometer

Water

Burning food sample

a) **i)** Write down **one** safety precaution that the student should take when doing this experiment.

.... [1]

ii) What did the student do to try and make their experiment a fair test?

.... [1]

b) Here are the student's results.

Food	Temperature of the water at the start (°C)	Temperature of the water at the end (°C)	Change in temperature (°C)
biscuit	19	42	23
bread	20	38	18
crisps	21	45	
pastry	19	44	

i) Complete the table by filling in the missing changes in temperature. [2]

ii) Which food contained the most energy? Explain how you worked out your answer.

....

....

.... [2]

iii) The student's teacher said that they should have measured the mass of each of the foods in their experiment.

Explain why that would have helped them make a more complete conclusion.

....

....

.... [2]

2 Bella sets up this experiment
to investigate the effect of amylase on
starch at different temperatures.

This is Bella's method:

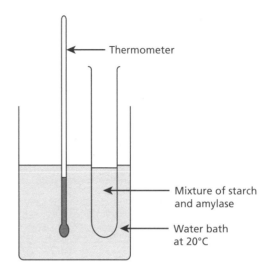

- Take a drop of the mixture out of the test
  tube every minute and test it for starch.

- Record how long it takes before the
  mixture tests negative for starch.

- Repeat the experiment with the
  water bath at different temperatures.

a) How would Bella test the mixture for starch?

....

.... [2]

b) Suggest a reason why Bella used a water bath rather than heating the mixture directly
with a Bunsen burner.

....

.... [1]

c) The table shows Bella's results.

Temperature (°C)	Time to get a negative test for starch (minutes)
20	10
30	4
40	2
50	6
60	10

i) Why did the mixture test negative for starch after a certain time?

....

.... [2]

ii) At which temperature did amylase work fastest? .... °C [1]

iii) What is the independent variable in Bella's experiment?

.... [1]

Total Marks .... / 15

Science in Use

1 Read the passage about macadamia nuts and answer the questions on the next page.

Macadamia nuts are an important food in Australia.

The nuts are very high in lipids but not the type that causes heart disease. They are low in carbohydrates but contain good amounts of protein, calcium and iron.

The demand for the nuts in Australia is so high that 4.5 million trees are grown in the country. However, can producing this much food be sustainable?

Growers have tried to make growing macadamia trees more sustainable in three different ways:

- Firstly, farmers try to limit how much carbon dioxide is released by making sure that there are local factories for processing the nuts.

  This means that the nuts do not have to travel far from the tree to be shelled, dried and packed.

- Secondly, farmers try to make sure that every part of the nut is reused or recycled.

  One factory can produce about 10 000 tonnes of waste shells each year. These shells are burned in power stations to generate electricity.

- Thirdly, farmers have tried to reduce the use of chemicals to control pests and diseases of the trees.

  One example is the use of a wasp to kill insects that bore into the trees.

a) Macadamia nuts are thought to be a healthy food.

How do the contents of the nuts explain each of the following features?

i) They provide large amounts of energy.

.... [1]

ii) They help with growth.

.... [1]

iii) They help prevent people getting anaemia.

.... [1]

b) Suggest why having local processing factories for the nuts means that less carbon dioxide is released.

....

....

.... [2]

c) Explain why burning nut shells to generate electricity is more sustainable than burning coal.

....

....

.... [2]

Total Marks .... / 7

	Vocabulary Builder	Maths Skills	Testing Understanding	Working Scientifically	Science in Use
Total Marks	.... / 17	.... / 8	.... / 40	.... / 15	.... / 7

Vocabulary Builder

1 Match the type of chemical reaction to its description.

Key word	Definition

Key word	Definition
Oxidation	Using heat to break down a substance into simpler substances
Electrolysis	Oxygen is added to a substance
Thermal decomposition	When a fuel combines with oxygen
Combustion	Using electricity to break down a substance into simpler substances
Reduction	Oxygen is removed from a substance

[4]

2 Complete the sentences about metal extraction using the words from the box. You can use the words once, more than once or not at all.

compound	element	pure	ores
native	reduction	oxidation	

Some metals like gold are not reactive and are found as _____ elements.

But most metals are reactive and are found in a _____ trapped inside rocks.

_____ are rocks that contain enough metal to make it worthwhile extracting

the _____ metal from them. Ores undergo _____ reactions

to extract the metal from its compound.

[5]

3 Methane is found in natural gas that is piped to many homes in the UK. Natural gas is combusted in boilers to convert the chemical energy store in the fuel to thermal energy store for cooking and to heat the house.

The word equation for this combustion reaction is given below:

methane + oxygen ⟶ carbon dioxide + water

a) What are the names of the reactants? .... [1]

b) What are the names of the products? .... [1]

c) What is the name of the fuel? .... [1]

d) What is the name of an element in this reaction? .... [1]

e) What are the names of the compounds in this reaction?

.... [1]

f) What is the name of the hydrocarbon in this reaction? .... [1]

4 All metals have some physical properties in common.

Match the name of the metal property with its definition. [3]

Metal property		Definition
Conductor		Bends easily
Sonorous		Makes a ringing noise when hit
Ductile		Allows heat and electricity to easily pass through
Malleable		Can be drawn into wires

Total Marks .... / 18

Maths Skills

1 The halogens are non-metal elements. The bar chart below shows the melting points of the first four halogen elements measured in °C.

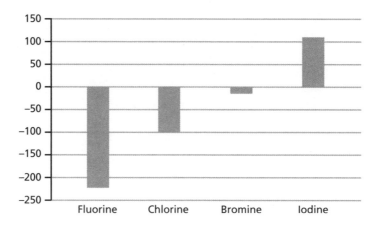

a) Label the x-axis and the y-axis. [3]

b) What is the name of the halogen with a melting point of −7 °C? [1]

c) What is the pattern in melting point as you go down group 7 of the periodic table?

[1]

2 The pie chart shows which elements are found in the Earth's crust.

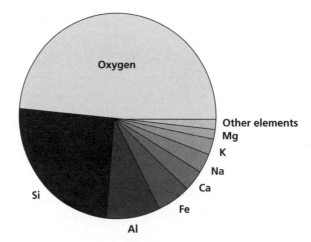

a) Which is the most common element in the Earth's crust? [1]

b) Approximately what percentage of the Earth's crust is made from silicon?

% [1]

c) Which is the most common metal in the Earth's crust? [1]

3 A sample of malachite was found to have 58% copper. One kilogram of malachite costs £244 and can undergo processing to extract the copper that can be sold for £16.

a) What mass of copper is there in 1 kg of malachite? Show your working and give the units in your answer.

mass = _____ [3]

b) Was this malachite an ore? Explain your answer.

....

.... [2]

Total Marks _____ / 13

Testing Understanding

1 Below is part of the periodic table. Use this to answer the following questions.

					H												He
Li												C			F		
	Mg										Al				Cl		
K			Ti			Fe											

a) Give the symbols of two elements in the same group.

.... [1]

b) Give the symbols of two elements in the same period.

.... [1]

c) Give the symbol of an alkali metal. .... [1]

d) Give the symbol of a halogen. .... [1]

e) Give the symbol of a noble gas. .... [1]

2 The table below contains the formulae of common substances. Complete the table by filling in the blank spaces.

Name	Formula	Number of elements present	Total number of atoms present
Water		2	
	SO_2		3
	PbO	2	
Calcium chloride			3

[8]

3 In Brazil, ethanol is used as a fuel in car engines. The ethanol reacts with oxygen in the air to make carbon dioxide and water.

a) What type of chemical reaction happens in the car engine? .... [1]

b) Write a word equation for the reaction in the car engine.

.... [3]

c) What simple laboratory test could be done to show carbon dioxide is made in this reaction?

....

....

.... [4]

4 Look at the following statements and decide if they are generally true for metals or generally true for non-metals. Put **one** tick in each row to show your answer.

Statement	Metals	Non-metals
On the left and centre of the periodic table		
Solids at room temperature		
Gases at room temperature		
Malleable		
Oxides are acidic		
Oxides are basic		

[6]

5 Bryony was investigating copper and found out that it had many everyday uses.

Suggest which properties make copper suitable for each use:

a) Cooking pans .... [1]

b) Electrical wires .... [1]

c) Plumbing pipes .... [1]

6 Ros was investigating how mass changed as 2.3g of magnesium ribbon was completely reacted with 1.6g oxygen to form magnesium oxide.

a) What is the name of the chemical reaction that Ros is investigating? .... [1]

b) Write a word equation for this reaction.

.... [3]

c) What mass of magnesium oxide would be formed? .... [1]

Total Marks .... / 35

1 Derek was investigating which strips of materials conducted electricity and which did not. He used the simple circuit shown in the diagram below.

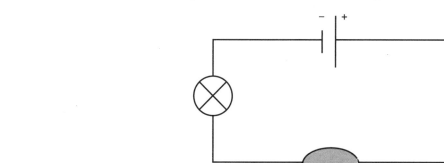

(Tested material)

a) What is the independent variable in Derek's experiment?

.... [1]

b) How would Derek know that a material was a conductor?

.... [1]

c) How could Derek keep the testing material in the simple circuit?

.... [1]

d) What is likely to be the main safety risk in this experiment?

....

.... [1]

e) Silicon is a metalloid. Predict and explain what would happen if Derek tested silicon in this experiment.

....

.... [2]

2 Kabir was investigating how the mass changed in a chemical reaction between calcium and water. He used the equipment in the diagram below.

a) What is the name of the glassware labelled A? .... [1]

b) What is the name of the measuring equipment labelled B? .... [1]

c) What is the independent variable in Kabir's experiment? .... [1]

d) What would happen to the mass reading? Explain your answer.

....

....

.... [3]

3 Daisy's science teacher showed her class the reaction between water and three corrosive metals – lithium, sodium and potassium.

a) Why are these metals kept in a jar of oil?

_____

_____ [2]

b) What safety precautions should the teacher make when preparing the metals to add them to the water?

_____

_____ [2]

c) All three metals floated when they were put into the water trough.

What does this tell us about the density of these metals?

_____ [1]

d) Universal indicator was added to the water trough at the end of the experiment.

What colour did the indicator go? Explain your answer.

_____

_____ [2]

4 Dimitri Mendeleev was the first person to suggest the periodic table. Although we do not use Mendeleev's original periodic table, we use a very similar one.

a) How did Mendeleev order the elements in his original periodic table?

_____

_____ [1]

b) How was Mendeleev's periodic table different from the other ways that the elements had been listed by other scientists like John Dalton?

_____

_____ [1]

c) How is the modern periodic table different to Mendeleev's original one?

_____

_____ [2]

5 Nikita was investigating the thermal decomposition of calcium carbonate to make limewater. She used the equipment in the diagrams below.

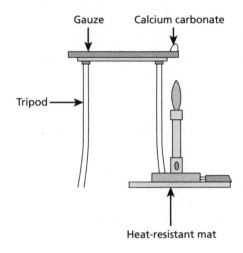

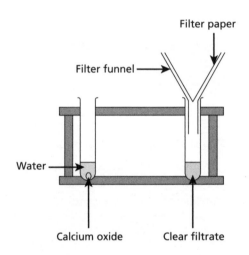

Describe the main stages of the experiment.

....

....

....

....

....

....

[5]

Total Marks .... / 28

1 Read the passage about the element carbon then answer the questions that follow.

Carbon is an element that can form more than one structure at room temperature. Each structure has the atoms arranged differently and this gives them different properties.

In diamond, the atoms have a crystalline structure where each atom bonds strongly to four carbon atoms. So, diamond is hard with a high melting point.

But carbon can also make sheets, where each atom is bonded to just three carbon atoms. One sheet is a material called graphene, which is so thin it is transparent. Many sheets of graphene layered on top of each other is graphite, which is the substance that makes the lead used in pencils. The layers slide easily over each other and leave a mark on the paper. Both graphene and graphite easily conduct electricity. Sheets of graphene can even roll up to make nanotubes which are very strong for their size.

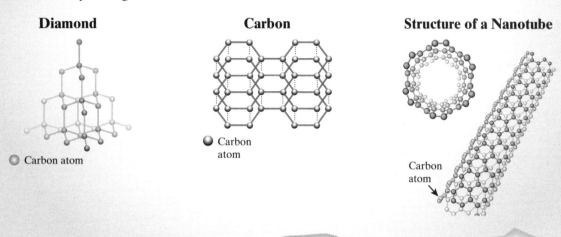

a) Which structure of carbon forms crystals? .... [1]

b) Which structures of carbon are transparent? .... [2]

c) What is the symbol for carbon? .... [1]

d) What group of the periodic table is carbon in? .... [1]

e) What period of the periodic table is carbon in? .... [1]

f) What is the atomic number of carbon? .... [1]

2 Read the passage about discovery of metals then answer the questions that follow.

In early history, mankind could only use any unreactive metals that they could find. But, as technology advanced, humans moved from the Stone Age (where they were only able to use wood, stone and materials from animals) to the Bronze Age (where they could forge metal into weapons and tools).

Bronze is a mixture of copper and tin. Both copper and tin are metals that can be extracted from minerals that contain the metal compounds using carbon in a hot fire.

a) What is the symbol for tin? .... [1]

b) Where on the periodic table would you find copper?

.... [2]

c) What colour would the flames be when copper is being extracted from its compound?

.... [1]

d) What is the chemical reaction used to extract the metal from its compound?

.... [1]

Total Marks .... / 12

	Vocabulary Builder	Maths Skills	Testing Understanding	Working Scientifically	Science in Use
Total Marks	/ 18	/ 13	/ 35	/ 28	/ 12

Vocabulary Builder

1 **a)** Draw a line to match each key word/term to its definition.

Key word/term	Definition

Atom	More than one substance not chemically joined
A molecule of an element	More than one type of atom joined together
A molecule of a compound	All the atoms are the same
A mixture of two elements	The smallest particle that can exist on its own

[3]

b) Draw a line to match each key word/term to its particle diagram.

Key word/term	Diagram
Atom	◯
A molecule of an element	◯⬤
A molecule of a compound	◯◯
A mixture of two elements	◯ ⬤

[3]

2 Complete the sentences about dissolving using the words from the box. You can use the words once, more than once or not at all.

dissolve	solute	solvent	solution	pure	mixture

Sugar .... is made when sugar is mixed with water. ....

water contains only water molecules and can dissolve sugar. Water is called the

.... and sugar is the .... [4]

3 Willow wanted to separate sand from water. She collected her sample and used a separating technique, as shown here.

a) What is the name of this separating technique?

.... [1]

b) What is the name of the equipment used to collect the filtrate?

.... [1]

c) What is the name of the equipment that holds the filter paper?

.... [1]

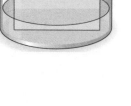

4 Asana was using a measuring cylinder to accurately measure 25.0 cm³ of water. Asana noticed that the water curved downwards in the measuring cylinder.

What is the name given to this observation? .... [1]

5 Zac was interested in investigating the colours of inks and dye. He was using the apparatus shown on the right in his investigation.

a) What is the name of this separation technique?

.... [1]

b) What is the name of the result of this separation technique?

.... [1]

c) R_f can be calculated. What does R_f mean?

.... [1]

Total Marks .... / 17

1. Juliette developed a chromatogram.

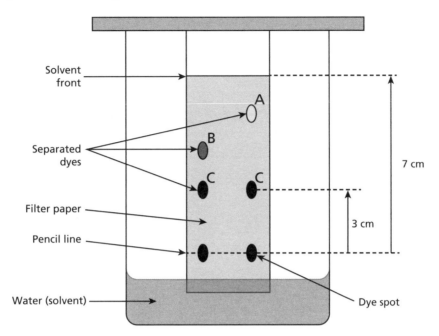

a) Use the chromatogram to determine the distance the solvent moved up the paper.

_____ [1]

b) Using the formula below, calculate the retardation factor (R_f) for the black pigment, C.
   Show your working and give your answer to 2 decimal places.

   R_f = distance moved by dye ÷ distance moved by solvent

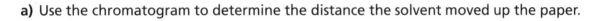

retardation factor = _____ [2]

c) The R_f value for the light grey pigment, A, was 0.85.

   Calculate the distance the dye moved up the paper. Show your working.

distance dye moved = _____ [2]

d) Suggest the R_f values for the green dyes that did not move from the pencil line.

_____ [1]

2 The composition of air has been unchanged for about 200 million years. This data can be shown in a diagram.

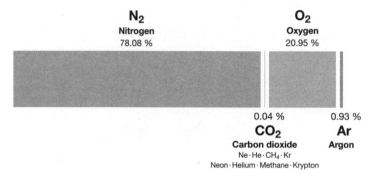

a) What is the percentage of air that is nitrogen?

.... % [1]

b) What is the approximate fraction of air that is oxygen?

.... [1]

c) What is the ratio of nitrogen to oxygen molecules in the air?

.... [1]

d) How many atoms of nitrogen are in a nitrogen molecule?

.... [1]

e) How many elements are in a molecule of carbon dioxide?

.... [1]

3 Imogen decided to look up the solubility of different sugars. She recorded her results in a scientific table.

Sugar	Solubility (g/100 g water)
Glucose	90
Fructose	40
Lactose	18.9

a) Which sugar has the highest solubility?

.... [1]

b) Draw a bar chart of these data on the graph paper below.

[5]

Total Marks .... / 17

Testing Understanding

1 **a)** Mixtures are made of substances that are not chemically joined.

Match the separating technique to the description of what it can separate.

Separation technique	What it separates
Filtering	Two immiscible liquids
Distillation	A solute from a solution
Chromatography	A solvent from a solution
Crystallisation	Insoluble solids from a liquid
Separating funnel	Inks and dyes

[4]

b) Otis was given a sample of sand mixed with brine. Describe how Otis could get a sample of the clean dry salt from this mixture.

....

....

.... [3]

2 A student was asked to purify a sample of water-soluble ink. She used distillation.

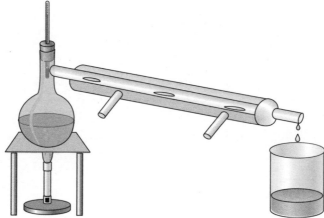

a) Which two physical processes happen during distillation?

.... [2]

b) What would be the temperature on the thermometer after the mixture had been boiling for some time?

.... °C [1]

c) How would you describe the colourless liquid collected?

.... [2]

d) What process would the student need to use to find out how many different colours make up the ink?

.... [1]

3 a) Classify the following as properties of **elements**, **compounds** or **mixtures**. Some statements can relate to more than one category.

　　i) Pure　　　　　　　　　　　　　　　　.. [2]

　　ii) Have a specific melting and boiling point　.. [2]

　　iii) Melt and boil over a range of temperatures　.. [1]

b) Classify the following as examples of **elements**, **compounds** or **mixtures**. Some statements can relate to more than one category.

　　i) Air　　　　　　　　　　　　　　　　　　.. [1]

　　ii) Water　　　　　　　　　　　　　　　　.. [1]

　　iii) Oxygen　　　　　　　　　　　　　　　.. [1]

Total Marks .... / 21

1 Jamie was given a mixture of soluble blue copper sulfate crystals and insoluble soot. She was asked to separate the two powders. She took the following steps.

1. Added water to the mixture and stirred it.

2. Filtered it.

3. Collected and dried the residue.

4. Collected the filtrate and evaporated the water.

a) In step 1, she noticed that the water turned blue. What had happened to make the water turn blue?

.... [1]

b) What was collected in step 3? Explain your answer.

....

.... [2]

c) What was formed in step 4? .... [1]

d) What piece of equipment would Jamie use to measure the mass of the substances collected?

.... [1]

2 **a)** Sonya was adding water to an ink bottle. But accidently, she added too much water into the bottle. She decided to use distillation to remove some of the water from the ink. Sonya used the equipment below. Add labels to name the key pieces of equipment in the diagram.

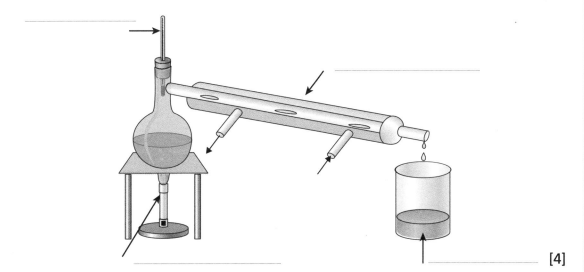

[4]

b) Suggest the temperature on the thermometer. .... °C [1]

c) Explain why the bulb of the thermometer must be in line with the side arm.

.... [2]

3 Naveed decided to investigate if the colour on his favourite red sweet was pure or a mixture. He chose to use chromatography with water in his investigation.

a) Complete the diagram by labelling A, B and C using the words from the box below. [3]

solution	solvent	solute	paper

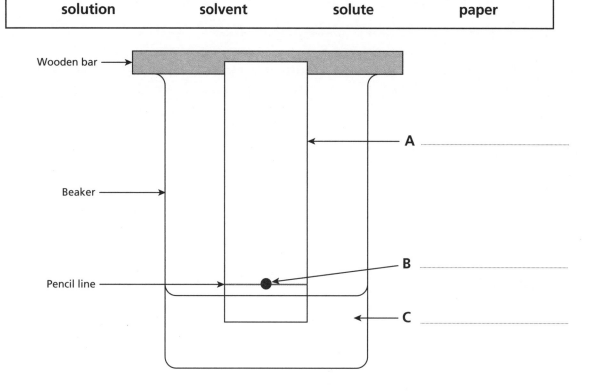

Wooden bar

A ....

Beaker

B ....

Pencil line

C ....

b) Explain why it is important that pencil is used rather than pen on the chromatogram.

.... [1]

c) Describe the appearance of the chromatogram if:

i) the red food colouring is pure

.... [1]

ii) the red food colouring is a mixture

.... [1]

iii) the red food colouring is insoluble in water.

.... [1]

Total Marks .... / 19

1 Humans are about 60% water and we need to drink daily. If we don't, we risk getting ill with dehydration and in extreme cases we would die. But water is a finite resource, and with climate change affecting rainfall and water tables it is becoming more difficult for us to have a safe and reliable supply of drinking water for everyone in the world.

In the UK, fresh water is processed to make it safe to drink. That water is then pumped to our homes for us to use from the tap.

The steps for making drinking water in the UK are:

1. Choose water supply low in soluble pollutants.
2. Remove insoluble solids from the water.
3. Remove pathogens by adding chlorine or ozone.
4. Fluoride is added to improve dental health.

a) What separation technique would you use in step 2?

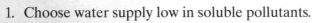 [1]

b) In the space below, draw a labelled diagram of the equipment you could use in a laboratory to model step 2.

[4]

c) Why is chlorine or ozone added to drinking water?

.... [1]

d) What are the health benefits of adding fluoride to drinking water?

.... [1]

e) Drinking water is not pure water.

Explain why drinking water is not pure water.

....

.... [2]

f) Name **one** separation technique that could be used to make pure water from fresh water.

.... [1]

Total Marks .... / 10

	Vocabulary Builder	Maths Skills	Testing Understanding	Working Scientifically	Science in Use
Total Marks	.... / 17	.... / 17	.... / 21	.... / 19	.... / 10

Vocabulary Builder

1 A model glider can fly a short distance through the air.

Use the words in the box to complete the sentences.

lift force	weight	air resistance

The force trying to slow the glider is the _____. The force helping to keep

the plane in the air is the _____. The force pulling the glider towards the

ground is the _____. [3]

2 Which object is made from an **elastic** material? Tick **one** box.

Piece of modelling clay ☐ Rubber band ☐ Glass beaker ☐ [1]

3 A spring can be stretched or squashed. Use the words in the box to complete the sentences.

compressive	bending	pulling	resistive

A spring can be stretched by a _____ force. A spring can be squashed

by a _____ force. [2]

4 The statements **A–F** give examples of forces in action.

A Opening a door   **B** A stone falling to the ground

C Warming hands by rubbing them   **D** A cyclist stopping at traffic lights
together

E A train pulling out of a station   **F** A barge going along a canal at a steady speed

Choose letters **A–F** as an example of each of the following:

a) Friction   _____   **b)** Braking force   _____

c) Moment   _____   **d)** Balanced forces   _____ [4]

5 **a)** Name the device that can be used to measure the force of gravity acting on a toy car.

_____ [1]

b) Write the name of the unit used in measuring this force.   _____ [1]

c) What is the symbol for the unit of force? Tick **one** box.

kg ☐   g ☐   N ☐   [1]

6 A toy car on the schoolroom floor is given a quick push. The car travels a short distance and then stops. Name **two** resistive forces that make the car slow down.

.... and .... [2]

7 A plank of wood can be used to lift a boulder. Read the sentences and write down if each one is **true** or **false**.

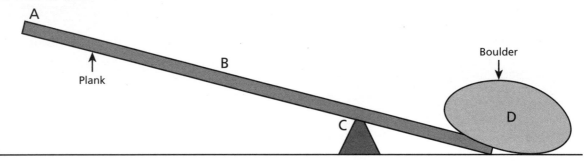

a) The weight of the boulder acts downwards from D. .... [1]

b) The fulcrum is at B. .... [1]

c) The fulcrum is at C. .... [1]

d) The plank is acting as a lever. .... [1]

e) A downward force at A creates a smaller moment than
   the same force applied at B. .... [1]

f) Pushing down on the plank at A turns the plank anticlockwise. .... [1]

8 The diagram shows a spring clamped at one end. The other end of the spring is pulled. The spring obeys Hooke's Law.

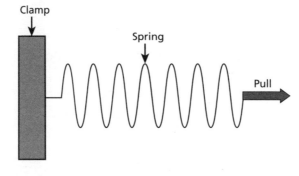

Tick the statement that describes Hooke's Law.

Pulling stretches the spring. ☐

If the pulling force is doubled the stretch doubles. ☐

If the pulling force is doubled the stretch halves. ☐ [1]

Total Marks .... / 22

1 Amir is measuring the weight of a pebble using a newton-meter.
Another name for a newton-meter is a spring balance.

a) What is the weight of the pebble?

.... N   [1]

b) What is the biggest weight that this
newton-meter can measure?

.... N   [1]

c) What would happen to the newton-meter if a weight
of about twenty newton was attached to the hook?

....

....

....

....   [1]

2 Diagram 1 shows a spring that has not been stretched. Diagram 2 shows the same spring
that has been pulled by a 10 N force. The spring follows Hooke's Law.

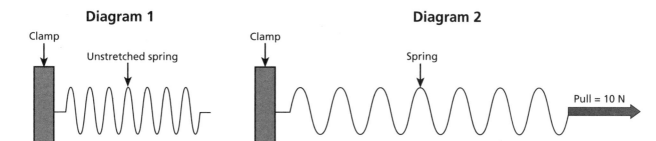

Diagram 1   Clamp   Unstretched spring   20 cm

Diagram 2   Clamp   Spring   Pull = 10 N   35 cm

a) How much has the spring **increased** in length?   .... cm   [1]

b) What would be the increase in length if the pulling force
had been 20 N?   .... cm   [1]

c) What would be the full length of the spring if the
pulling force had been 20 N?   .... cm   [1]

d) When the pulling force is removed, the spring goes back to its original length.

What is the name given to this type of behaviour?

....   [1]

3) The diagram shows a container on the floor. A child pushes the container with a force of 10 N. There is a friction force of 10 N between the container and the floor.

What happens to the container? Tick **one** box.

The container moves towards the door. ☐

The container does not move. ☐

The container moves away from the door. ☐ [1]

4) A skydiver is in freefall and has not yet opened her parachute. Her weight is 600 N. The air resistance acting on her is 500 N.

What is happening to the skydiver's speed? Tick **one** box.

Increasing ☐

Decreasing ☐

Not changing ☐ [1]

5) On the surface of the Earth, the force of gravity on a 1 kg mass is 10 N.

a) What would be the force of gravity on a 2 kg mass? _____ N [1]

b) What would be the force of gravity on a 5 kg mass? _____ N [1]

c) On the surface of the Moon, the force of gravity of a 1 kg mass is 1.6 N.

What does this tell us about gravity on the Moon?

_____ [1]

6 A car travels a distance of 50 km in 2 hours. The equation to calculate speed is:

speed = distance ÷ time

a) Calculate the average speed of the car in km/hour.

.... km/h [1]

b) The driver then decides to continue his journey for one more hour. During this hour the car travels 22 km.

Calculate the average speed for the whole journey. .... km/h [1]

7 A plumber uses a spanner to loosen a tight bolt. The table shows three spanners of different lengths. The plumber applies the same size force to the end of each spanner.

Spanner	Length (cm)
A	10
B	15
C	20

a) Which spanner would create the biggest turning effect? Tick **one** box.

A ☐   B ☐   C ☐   [1]

b) What is the other name for the turning effect of a force?

.... [1]

8 Yousef makes a model see-saw using a one metre rule. He uses a triangular piece of wood as the fulcrum. The points X, A, B and C are marked on the metre rule.

X   A   B   C

Metre rule →

← Fulcrum

a) Yousef places a mass of weight 2 N at point X on the rule causing the rule to turn.

Does the rule turn clockwise or anticlockwise?

.... [1]

b) To balance the rule again, Yousef puts a mass of weight 1 N on the right-hand side of the rule.

At which point on the rule should Yousef put this mass? Tick **one** box.

A ☐   B ☐   C ☐   [1]

Total Marks .... / 18

Testing Understanding

1 A bungee is made from an elastic material. Explain what this means.

....

.... [2]

2 Three newton-meters, labelled A, B and C, are shown below.

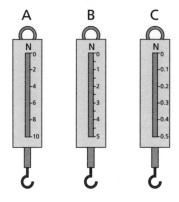

Maria estimates the weight of a pebble to be somewhere between 2 and 4N.

Which newton-meter should she use to get the most accurate measurement of the pebble's weight? Explain your answer.

....

....

.... [3]

3 When mass M is attached to the spring, it stretches the spring and then stops moving.

There are two forces acting on mass M and they are now balanced.

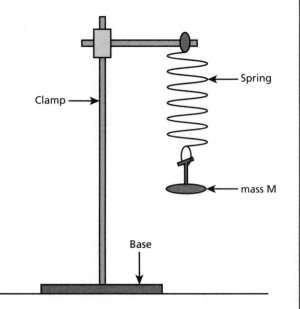

a) What object exerts an upward force on mass M?

.... [1]

b) What object exerts a downward force on mass M?

.... [1]

4 A rocket has just been launched. It is moving faster and faster away from the Earth's surface. One of the forces acting on the rocket has been labelled in the diagram below.

Direction rocket is moving

Engine driving force

a) Name the **two** other forces acting on the rocket.

.... and .... [2]

b) Which one of the three forces is the largest? Explain your answer.

....

....

....

.... [2]

5 A teacher thinks that a spring might have been damaged by having too much weight attached to it. If the spring is undamaged, then doubling the weight attached to the spring should double the amount of stretch.

The teacher asks a student in the class to test the spring to see if it is undamaged.

Half metre rule

Spring

Clamp

Base

a) Write some instructions telling the student how to measure the stretch caused by a 1 N weight.

....

....

....

....

.... [4]

b) The student's measurements are shown below.

Total weight attached to the spring (N)	Stretch in the spring (cm)
1	5
2	15

Use the data to decide if the spring has been damaged.
Explain your answer.

....

....

.... [3]

6 A model train takes 20 s to travel around its track. The length of the track is 4 m.
Calculate the speed of the train in centimetres per second. Show all your working out.

speed = _____ cm/s   [3]

7 The table gives distance and time measurements for different journeys made by three different vehicles.

Vehicle	Journey distance (km)	Journey time (hours)
Car	100	2
Motorbike	60	1
Van	40	1

Which vehicle had the greatest average speed? Explain your answer.

_____

_____   [2]

8 A home owner has chosen a new front door for his house. He cannot decide whether to have the door handle fitted near the edge of the door (Diagram A) or in the middle (Diagram B).

Once fitted, the door is shut from the outside by pulling on the door handle.

Which diagram shows the best position for the door handle to make it easiest to shut the door when leaving the house? Explain your answer.

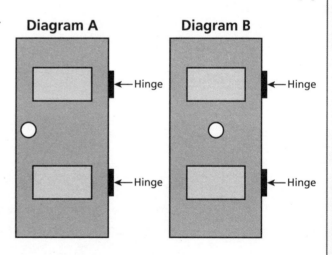

_____

_____

_____   [3]

Total Marks _____ / 26

Working Scientifically

1 Diagram A shows a block of wood in the shape of a cube. Different materials are attached to three of its sides.

Skylah uses the apparatus shown in Diagram B to test which material has the largest friction when in contact with a steel sheet. She adds masses to the hanger until the cube slips forward. The larger the mass needed to move the cube, the bigger the friction between the material and the steel sheet.

Diagram A

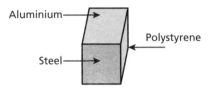

Diagram B

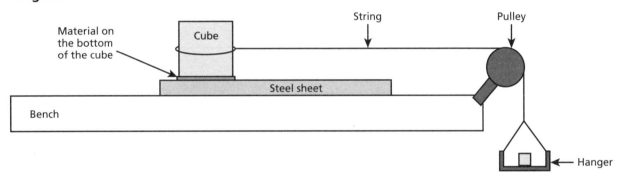

Skylah's measurements are given in the table below.

Material moving across the steel sheet	Mass added/g	Mass of hanger/g	Total mass/g pulling the cube
Polystyrene	35	10	
Aluminium	60	10	
Steel	70	10	
Steel coated with oil	10	10	

a) Complete the last column of the table. [4]

b) Which material produced the most friction in contact with the steel sheet?

.... [1]

c) Did the oil act as a **lubricant** between the steel on the cube and the steel sheet? Explain your answer.

....

.... [2]

d) The materials being tested were stuck to the same cube.

Why was this better than having the materials stuck to different cubes?

....

.... [1]

Total Marks .... / 8

Science in Use

1 Read the passage and then answer the questions.

The Airbus A350 is a long-range aircraft that can carry 350 passengers. It is 67 m long, which is about the length of three tennis courts. It has a weight of 2 700 000 N. The Airbus has two engines. Each engine provides 350 000 N of thrust. Its wings have a special shape called an aerofoil. As its engines drive the Airbus along the runway, the flow of air across the wings creates a lift force. Increasing the speed of the Airbus makes the lift force increase. When a speed of 1000 km per hour is reached, the lift force is big enough for the aircraft to take off. When the Airbus has reached its usual high altitude, it cruises at a steady speed of about 900 km per hour.

a) What is the total driving force generated by the engines of the Airbus A350?

driving force = ... N [1]

b) What size of lift force is needed to just lift the Airbus off the ground? Tick **one** box. [1]

270 N ☐   2700 N ☐   270 000 N ☐   2 700 000 N ☐

c) What distance in km does the Airbus travel in two hours when it is cruising at high altitude?

distance = ... km   [1]

d) The diagram shows the aircraft cruising at a high altitude.

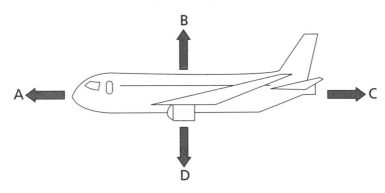

Identify the four forces acting on the aircraft. Select either A, B, C or D:

weight: ....   air resistance: ....

engine driving force: ....   lift: ....   [4]

e) Complete the sentences using words from the box.

increase	decrease	constant

As the Airbus's speed increases as it travels along the runway, the lift force will

.... When the Airbus is cruising at a constant speed, the air resistance

is .... When the aircraft lands on the runway, the engines are put into

reverse to .... the aircraft's speed. When the aircraft lands, its brakes

are applied to its wheels to .... the friction between the wheels and

the runway.   [4]

Total Marks .... / 11

	Vocabulary Builder	Maths Skills	Testing Understanding	Working Scientifically	Science in Use
Total Marks	.... / 22	.... / 18	.... / 26	.... / 8	.... / 11

Vocabulary Builder

1 Complete the sentences using words from the box.

| kinetic | chemical | thermal |

a) A cup of hot tea has a greater store of _____ energy than a cup of cold tea. [1]

b) A fast-moving car has a greater store of _____ energy than a slow-moving car of the same mass. [1]

c) A 2 kg bag of sugar has a greater store of _____ energy than a 1 kg bag of sugar. [1]

d) A boy's hands are cold so he rubs them together transferring _____ energy stored in his muscles to the _____ energy of his hands. [2]

e) When a moving car's brakes are applied, _____ energy of the car's wheels is transferred to _____ energy in the brakes. [2]

f) As a car pulls away from traffic lights, its store of _____ energy decreases, and its store of _____ energy increases. [2]

2 When a force moves, the energy transferred is called **work**. Consider a car breaking down and the passengers then pushing the car nearer to the kerb. The push applied by the passengers moves the car, so work is being done.

Which of these activities causing energy transfer involves doing work? Circle either **Yes** or **No**.

a) Pushing a shopping trolley along the aisle at the supermarket.   Yes   No   [1]

b) Trying to lift an object that is too heavy to be moved.   Yes   No   [1]

c) Warming your hands on a hot cup of coffee.   Yes   No   [1]

3 A man is pushing his child in a pushchair at a steady speed along the pavement. Read the sentences and write down if each one is **true** or **false**.

The man is doing work. _____ [1]

The man's store of chemical energy in his muscles is decreasing. _____ [1]

The pushchair's store of kinetic energy is increasing. _____ [1]

4 The image shows a catapult about to launch a toy rocket. The rubber band on the catapult has been stretched, creating a store of elastic potential energy.

What happens to the stores of energy as the catapult is released?

_____

_____

_____ [2]

5 A tennis player throws a ball vertically up into the air. Complete the sentences using the terms in the box.

kinetic	gravitational potential	work

In throwing the ball, the tennis player does _____ and transfers

_____ energy to the ball. As the ball moves upwards, its store of

_____ energy decreases and its store of _____ energy

increases until it reaches its maximum height. [4]

6 Hot tea is poured into a cold cup.

a) Describe what happens to the size of the thermal energy stores of the cup and the tea as time passes.

_____

_____ [2]

b) The energy transfer that occurs does not involve doing work.

What is it that drives the energy transfer between the tea and the cup?

_____ [1]

c) The tabletop beneath the cup becomes warmer.

What is the name of the process that transfers thermal energy into the tabletop?

_____ [1]

d) How will the thermal energy store of the air surrounding the cup change after the tea has been poured?

_____ [1]

7 The chemical energy stored in many cars is in the form of fuel. Complete the sentences.

a) Two common fuels used in cars are diesel and _____. [1]

b) Burning the fuel in the car's engine produces exhaust gases which

_____ the air. [1]

c) There are now more electric cars on our roads and these do not give out exhaust gases. But, some of the electrical energy for these cars is produced at a power station which burns

fossil fuels, such as _____, producing gases that cause climate

_____. [2]

8 When a tuning fork is hit on the bench, its prongs move rapidly back and forth, making a sound.

a) What is the name given to the motion of the tuning
fork's prongs? _____ [1]

b) What is the medium that carries the sound wave to
the ear? _____ [1]

c) How does the sound wave affect the person's eardrum?

_____ [1]

d) What type of wave is a sound wave?

_____ [1]

9 The diagram shows a loud speaker connected to a device which sends it an electric current.

Signal generator   Connecting
leads

Diaphragm

a) Complete the sentences.

The electric current makes the _____ of the loudspeaker vibrate. This

vibration makes the air _____ vibrate, creating a sound wave. If the

vibrations are speeded up, the sound has a higher _____. [3]

b) Write the name for the unit of frequency. .... [1]

c) Give the symbol for the unit of frequency. .... [1]

Maths Skills

1 When a force moves an object, energy is transferred. The amount of energy transferred is called **work**. Work can be calculated from the equation:

work = force × distance

a) Calculate the work done in each of the examples.

i) A pram is pushed with a force of 5 N along a pavement of length 20 m.

work done = ... J   [1]

ii) A shopping trolley is pushed with a force of 10 N along a supermarket aisle of length 25 m.

work done = ... J   [1]

iii) Lifting an object requires a force equal to the object's weight. A person lifts a box of weight 50 N from the floor onto a table 0.8 m high.

work done = ... J   [1]

iv) A person climbs up a ladder propped against a tree. The person is now 2 m above the ground. The person's weight is 600 N.

work done = ... J   [1]

b) Complete the sentence to describe the changes in energy stores in part **a) iv)**.

The store of .... energy in the person's muscles decreases and the

person's store of .... increases.   [2]

c) i) The lift in a tall building is raised by a cable exerting a force of 8000 N. The lift goes up 80 m. How much work is done?

work done = ... J   [1]

ii) Divide your answer to part **i)** by 1000 to obtain the work done in kilojoules.

work done = ... kJ   [1]

d) The engines of an aircraft provide a total driving force of 100 000 N. The aircraft travels along a runway of length 3000 m. How much work is done? Give your answer in J and kJ.

work done = ... J   [1]

work done = ... kJ   [1]

2 A gardener pushes down on a plank at point **A**, to try to lift a boulder.

Push

A

Boulder

Plank

B

a) The gardener is pushing down with a force of 400 N. The end of the plank at A moves down by a distance of 0.6 m.

How much work does he do?

work done = _____ J [1]

b) The boulder has a weight of 1200 N. Using the plank as a lever, the gardener is able to lift the boulder by applying a much smaller force.

Predict how high the plank can lift the boulder. Tick **one** box.

0.6 m ☐   1.0 m ☐   0.2 m ☐   [1]

3 The chemical energy stored in 1 g of petrol is 45 000 J. One litre of petrol has a mass of 800 g.

How much chemical energy is stored in one litre of petrol?

chemical energy = _____ J [1]

4 A 100 g bar of chocolate has a chemical energy store of 2200 kJ.

How much chemical energy is stored in 1 g of chocolate? Give your answer in kJ and J.

chemical energy = _____ kJ [1]

chemical energy = _____ J [1]

5 Maisie is trying to estimate the speed of a sound as it travels through air. She stands 150 m from the side of a high wall. She hits two blocks of wood together to make a loud sound. She estimates that the echo comes back to her in about 1 second.

Estimate the speed that sound travels through the air.

speed = _____ m/s [1]

6 Humans can hear sounds up to a frequency of about 20 kHz.

What is this frequency in Hz?

frequency = _____ Hz   [1]

Total Marks _____ / 17

Testing Understanding

1 Pushing a shopping trolley along an aisle at the supermarket is an example of doing work.

a) Which activity involves the most work? Tick **one** box.

Pushing an empty trolley halfway along the aisle. ☐

Pushing a full trolley along the full length of the aisle. ☐

Pushing an empty trolley along the full length of the aisle. ☐   [1]

b) Complete the sentences.

While you are pushing the trolley, the store of _____ energy in your

muscles decreases. As you push the trolley at a steady speed, you are doing work to

overcome friction, so the store of _____ energy in the trolley's

wheels increases.   [2]

2 A ramp is an example of a simple machine that can help make a job easier for us. In the diagram, the ramp is making it easier for Isla to load a heavy fridge into a van.

work = force × distance

a) The force needed to lift the fridge up into the van without using the ramp is 1000 N.

Calculate how much work would be done in lifting the fridge directly into the van.

work done = _____ J   [1]

b) The fridge is too heavy for Isla to lift directly into the van, so she uses the ramp.

Predict what force Isla applies to the fridge to push it up the ramp into the van. Tick **one** box.

1000 N ☐   1250 N ☐   125 N ☐   [1]

c) Read the sentences and write down if each one is **true** or **false**.

In getting the fridge into the van, chemical energy in Isla's muscles is transferred to gravitational potential energy. .... [1]

Isla would be doing the same amount of work whether she uses the ramp or not. .... [1]

Isla has to exert a greater force getting the fridge into the van when she uses the ramp. .... [1]

3 Samara picks a ball up off the ground and throws it upwards. The ball follows the path shown. She releases the ball at point **X**. It returns to the ground at point **Z**.

Choose either **X**, **Y** or **Z** to complete the sentences.

The ball has the most gravitational potential energy at point ....

The ball has the least gravitational potential energy at point ....

The ball has the most kinetic energy at point .... [3]

4 Starting at point **A**, a cyclist freewheels down a hill. The ground is rough so there is significant friction between the wheels and the ground. Between **A** and **B** his speed increases. From **B** to **C** his speed does not change. He comes to a stop at **D**.

a) Between which two points is the cyclist's kinetic energy increasing? Tick **one** box.

A to B ☐   B to C ☐   C to D ☐ [1]

b) By which point has all the cyclist's initial gravitational potential energy been transferred to thermal energy? Tick **one** box.

B ☐   C ☐   D ☐ [1]

c) Between which two points does the store of gravitational potential energy of the cyclist and his bicycle decrease by the same amount that the thermal energy store increases? Tick **one** box.

A to B ☐   B to C ☐   C to D ☐ [1]

5 The diagram shows an electric bell inside a sealed glass covered container. When a teacher connects the battery, the bell rings continuously. The hammer can be seen hitting the gong.

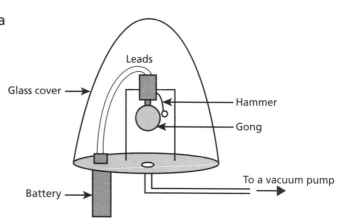

The teacher switches on the vacuum pump, which then starts to remove the air from the container. Jacob observes that the hammer keeps hitting the gong, but the sound is getting quieter and quieter. Explain Jacob's observation.

....

....

.... [3]

6 A buzzer is pressed to make a sound. The sound is detected first by microphone A then by microphone B. The microphones convert the energy transferred by the sound wave into an electrical signal.

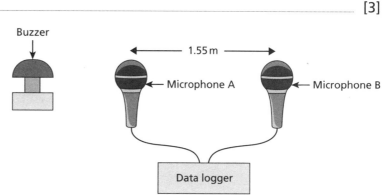

The data logger records the time interval between the electrical signals detected by the microphones. Time interval = 0.00453 s.

Calculate the speed of sound. Show your working.

speed = ... m/s   [2]

Total Marks .... / 19

Working Scientifically

1 In a scientific enquiry, Jade is comparing the thermal insulation properties of three solid materials – polystyrene beads, cotton wool balls and sawdust.

Polystyrene	**Cotton wool**	**Sawdust**

The apparatus Jade has set up is shown below.

Jade plans to put hot water in the inner beaker, and to then put polystyrene balls in the gap between the inner and outer beaker. She intends to measure the water temperature as time passes. She plans to repeat the procedure having filled the gap with cotton wool, and then with sawdust.

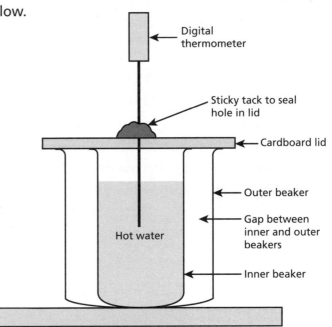

Digital thermometer

Sticky tack to seal hole in lid

Cardboard lid

Outer beaker

Gap between inner and outer beakers

Hot water

Inner beaker

a) To identify the best insulator, Jade wants to find out how quickly the water cools for each of the three insulators surrounding the inner beaker.

Explain why it is important that the three insulators have the same thickness. Also explain how the apparatus achieves this.

_____

_____

_____ [3]

b) Jade wants to put the same volume of water into the inner beaker for each of the three tests. She has a spare beaker and a measuring cylinder available, as shown below.

500 ml

She has decided to put 250 ml of hot water into the inner beaker. Should she use the spare beaker or the measuring cylinder when measuring out 250 ml of hot water? Explain your answer.

_____

_____

_____

_____

_____ [2]

c) For each of the three tests, Jade starts to record temperature measurements as the water temperature passes through 70°C. Her measurements are shown in the table.

Time (minutes)	Temperature in °C for polystyrene beads	Temperature in °C for cotton wool	Temperature in °C for sawdust
0	70	70	70
5	64	66	62
10	60.5	63	58
15	58	60.5	55
20	56	58	53
25	54	56.5	51
30	53	55	50

i) Fill in the table below to record the temperature fall for each material in 30 minutes.

Material	Temperature fall (°C)
polystyrene beads	
cotton wool	
sawdust	

[3]

ii) List the three materials in insulating order with the best insulator first.

1. .... 2. .... 3. .... [3]

d) Jade plots five of the temperature and time data for the polystyrene beads insulator on a graph.

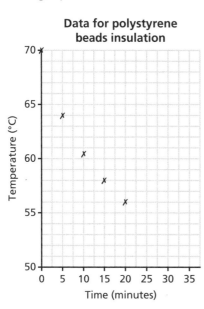

Data for polystyrene beads insulation

On the graph, plot the remaining two points and draw a single, curved line through all the points. [3]

e) As time passes, does the temperature drop more quickly or more slowly?

.... [1]

Science in Use

1 Read the passage and then answer the questions.

Probably two of the most important uses of sound are for communication and to enjoy as music. However, there are many other uses.

A sound wave creates a moving pattern of high and low pressure regions. So, a sound wave is also known as a **pressure wave**. Two applications of the pressure changes caused by sound are shown below:

Jewellery and equipment cleaner

Dental plaque remover

The jewellery and equipment cleaner contains a diaphragm, similar to that in a loudspeaker. The diaphragm produces sound waves of frequency 40 kHz. The changes in pressure caused by the sound wave clean pieces of jewellery or equipment by agitating the cleaning fluid.

The dental plaque remover has a tip that vibrates at a frequency of 37 kHz. The sound wave produced by the tip is directed at a patient's teeth by the dentist to remove plaque in order to keep the teeth healthy.

a) Give the range of human hearing.

from .... Hz to .... Hz   [2]

b) Explain what is meant by ultrasound.

.... [1]

c) Are the frequencies of the jewellery cleaner and the dental plaque remover classed as ultrasound? Explain your answer.

....

.... [2]

d) Ultrasound imaging is used to create a picture of something we cannot see directly, for example, the ultrasound scan of an unborn baby.

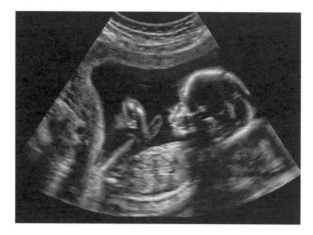

What property of sound waves enables the ultrasound scan to be produced?

.... [1]

e) The table gives the speed of sound through different materials at room temperature.

Material	Speed (m/s)
Steel	5790
Aluminium	3100
Water	1480
Air	331

Describe any trends in the data.

....

.... [2]

Total Marks .... / 8

	Vocabulary Builder	Maths Skills	Testing Understanding	Working Scientifically	Science in Use
Total Marks	.... / 39	.... / 17	.... / 19	.... / 15	.... / 8

The Periodic Table

Key

relative atomic mass
atomic symbol
name
atomic (proton) number

1	1	1	1	1	1	1	1
1							
H							
hydrogen							
1							

1	2											3	4	5	6	7	0
																	4 **He** helium 2
7 **Li** lithium 3	9 **Be** beryllium 4											11 **B** boron 5	12 **C** carbon 6	14 **N** nitrogen 7	16 **O** oxygen 8	19 **F** fluorine 9	20 **Ne** neon 10
23 **Na** sodium 11	24 **Mg** magnesium 12											27 **Al** aluminium 13	28 **Si** silicon 14	31 **P** phosphorus 15	32 **S** sulfur 16	35.5 **Cl** chlorine 17	40 **Ar** argon 18
39 **K** potassium 19	40 **Ca** calcium 20	45 **Sc** scandium 21	48 **Ti** titanium 22	51 **V** vanadium 23	52 **Cr** chromium 24	55 **Mn** manganese 25	56 **Fe** iron 26	59 **Co** cobalt 27	59 **Ni** nickel 28	63.5 **Cu** copper 29	65 **Zn** zinc 30	70 **Ga** gallium 31	73 **Ge** germanium 32	75 **As** arsenic 33	79 **Se** selenium 34	80 **Br** bromine 35	84 **Kr** krypton 36
85 **Rb** rubidium 37	88 **Sr** strontium 38	89 **Y** yttrium 39	91 **Zr** zirconium 40	93 **Nb** niobium 41	96 **Mo** molybdenum 42	[98] **Tc** technetium 43	101 **Ru** ruthenium 44	103 **Rh** rhodium 45	106 **Pd** palladium 46	108 **Ag** silver 47	112 **Cd** cadmium 48	115 **In** indium 49	119 **Sn** tin 50	122 **Sb** antimony 51	128 **Te** tellurium 52	127 **I** iodine 53	131 **Xe** xenon 54
133 **Cs** caesium 55	137 **Ba** barium 56	139 **La*** lanthanum 57	178 **Hf** hafnium 72	181 **Ta** tantalum 73	184 **W** tungsten 74	186 **Re** rhenium 75	190 **Os** osmium 76	192 **Ir** iridium 77	195 **Pt** platinum 78	197 **Au** gold 79	201 **Hg** mercury 80	204 **Tl** thallium 81	207 **Pb** lead 82	209 **Bi** bismuth 83	[209] **Po** polonium 84	[210] **At** astatine 85	[222] **Rn** radon 86
[223] **Fr** francium 87	[226] **Ra** radium 88	[227] **Ac*** actinium 89	[261] **Rf** rutherfordium 104	[262] **Db** dubnium 105	[266] **Sg** seaborgium 106	[264] **Bh** bohrium 107	[277] **Hs** hassium 108	[268] **Mt** meitnerium 109	[271] **Ds** darmstadtium 110	[272] **Rg** roentgenium 111							

Elements with atomic numbers 112–116 have been reported but not fully authenticated

*The Lanthanoids (atomic numbers 58–71) and the Actinoids (atomic numbers 90–103) have been omitted.

Cu and **Cl** have not been rounded to the nearest whole number.

Answers

Cells – the Building Blocks of Life

Pages 4–15

Vocabulary Builder

1.

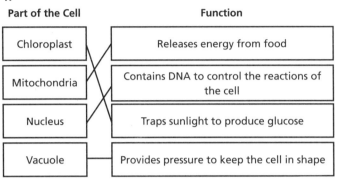

Part of the Cell	Function
Chloroplast	Releases energy from food
Mitochondria	Contains DNA to control the reactions of the cell
Nucleus	Traps sunlight to produce glucose
Vacuole	Provides pressure to keep the cell in shape

[3 marks if four or three correct; 2 marks if two correct; 1 mark if one correct]

2. a) root hair cell [1]
   b) bacterium [1]
   c) sperm cell [1]
   d) paramecium [1]
   e) nerve cell [1]
   f) euglena [1]
3. a) True, False [2]
   b) False, True [2]
   c) False, False [2]
   d) True, False [2]

Maths Skills

1. a)–b)

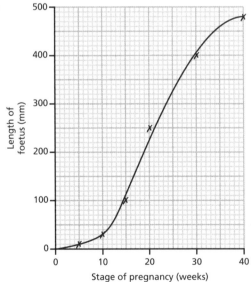

a) **[2 marks for all five points correctly plotted; 1 mark if only four points correctly plotted]**
b) **[1 mark for a smooth line drawn]**

> Remember, a curve of best fit does not actually need to go through the points.

c) 325 mm (+/– 5 mm) [1]
d) 15 to 20 weeks [1]

> The fastest growth is where the curve is steepest.

e) The length of foetus might be shorter. [1]
2. a) mitochondria [1]
   b) cheek cells and liver cells [1]
   c) ×2 [1]
   d) 10 micrometres [1]
   e) They are the same size. [1]

Testing Understanding

1. a) cells ⟶ tissues ⟶ organs ⟶ systems ⟶ organisms
   [1 mark for tissues before organs; 1 mark for organs before systems; 1 mark for systems before organisms]
   b) i) sperm – cell [1]
      ii) heart – organ [1]
      iii) bone – tissue [1]

> Be careful with these questions because bone and muscle are tissues, but a bone or a muscle are organs.

2.

Uses wind dispersal	Uses animal dispersal	Uses self-dispersal	Uses water dispersal
B, D	A, E	C	

[5]

3. a) Use a knife to cut a thin peel of onion tissue. [1]
   Place the tissue on the microscope slide. [1]
   Add a drop of stain. [1]
   Put a cover slip on top of the tissue. [1]
   b) To make some of the structures visible **[1]**; because the cell was transparent **[1]**
   c) i) **[1 mark for three cells drawn and correct shape. Plus 2 marks for any two labels from: nucleus; cell membrane; cytoplasm]**

> Remember in biological drawings, lines should be continuous and not sketchy. Also there should not be any shading.

   ii) **Any two from:** they would be smaller; they would not have a nucleus; they would have a cell wall [2]
4. a) petal = A **[1]**; ovule = F **[1]**; anther = B **[1]**; stigma = H **[1]**
   b) from B to H [2]
   c) F [1]
   d) anthers **[1]**; stigmas **[1]**; nectar/scent **[1]**
5. a) testis [1]
   b) It carries the sperm along the penis and into the female. [1]

c) It stops the sperm getting to the urethra/penis **[1]**; therefore, sperm cannot fertilise an egg **[1]**

d) i) day 2 **[1]**

   ii) 0.6 thousand million **[1]**

   iii) When it is warmer, sperm production drops **[1]**, being in the scrotum makes them cooler **[1]** so more sperm are made **[1]**.

6. a) i) P **[1]**

   ii) R **[1]**

b) i) Any three from: Q is the placenta; supplies the baby with nutrients; removes waste from the baby; makes hormones **[3]**

   ii) Any two from: V is the amniotic fluid; protects the baby; cushions the baby from shock **[2]**

Working Scientifically

1. a) Time / How long it takes to reach the ground **[1]**

> The independent variable is the factor that the experimenter changes and the dependent variable is the factor that is measured.

b) Any one from: fruits came from the same tree; all dropped from 2 metres **[1]**

c) i) 10 **[1]**

   ii) The longer the wing, the longer the fruit took to reach the ground. **[1]**

   iii) Any one from: Compare their conclusion with a trusted source/text book; time more than ten fruit to see if the same pattern is seen with a larger sample size. **[1]**

   iv) Draw around the wing on a piece of graph paper **[1]**; count the squares. **[1]**

Science in Use

1. a) 5% **[1]**

b) 15% of 200 **[1]**; 30 women **[1]**

c) i) blocked oviducts **[1]**

   ii) In IVF the eggs are removed from the ovaries and the embryo is put into the uterus **[1]**; so the blockage is bypassed. **[1]**

2. a) by eating them and passing them out in their faeces **[1]**; by getting them caught on their fur **[1]**.

b) If they cannot be dispersed, plants will be stuck in one area **[1]**; the weather/climate in that area might become unsuitable **[1]**.

c) Animals can move along the grass verges **[1]**; to new areas/habitats **[1]**.

Eating Drinking and Breathing

Pages 16–27

Vocabulary Builder

1. a) trachea **[1]**

b) diaphragm **[1]**

c) alveoli **[1]**

d) bronchioles **[1]**

2.

Disease	Cause
anaemia	lack of vitamin C
asthma	lack of iron
lung cancer	tightening of muscles in the bronchioles
rickets	chemicals in cigarette smoke
scurvy	lack of vitamin D

[4 marks if five or four correct; 3 marks if three correct; 2 marks if two correct; 1 mark if one correct]

3. a) True, True, False **[3]**

b) True, False, False **[3]**

c) False, False, True **[3]**

Maths Skills

1. a) 20% **[1]**

b)

[1 mark gained for each correct food group, up to 3 marks]

> There are 20 small sections on the pie chart so each one represents 5%.

c) i) 25 ÷ 5 **[1]**; 5 times greater **[1]**

   ii) The child in country B might grow faster **[1]**; because they eat more protein **[1]**.

Testing Understanding

1. a) i) 0.15 g **[1]**

   ii) Protein is needed for growth **[1]**; the 10-year-old is still growing **[1]**.

   iii) Add biuret reagent **[1]**; look for purple/violet colour **[1]**

> In food test questions, remember to include the name of the reagent and the colour seen if the test is positive.

b) Any two from: Her periods have not started yet; so she is not losing blood every month; she needs less iron to make new red blood cells **[2]**

> Remember that haemoglobin contains iron.

c) Any one from: red meat; liver; vegetables; beans; nuts; dried fruit **[1]**

2. a) i) Rubber sheet [1]
 ii) Balloons [1]
 iii) Tube A [1]
 b) **Any three from:** The balloons would inflate; because air would be drawn into tube A; because the volume would increase in the jar; so the pressure would decrease [3]
3. a) D [1]
 b) liver [1]
 c) E [1]
 d) By peristalsis [1]; as the muscles contract [1].
 e) It absorbs water [1]; making the waste more solid [1].
4. 12 [1]; 24 [1]; 0.6–0.7 [1]; carbon dioxide [1]
5. a) i) ii)

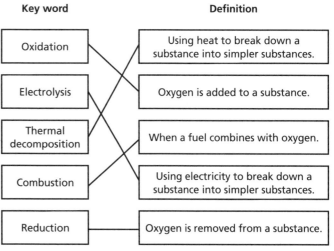

Wall of alveolus

Wall of blood vessel

Direction of blood flow

Oxygen

Carbon dioxide

Red blood cells

[1 mark for each labelled arrow, up to 2 marks]

> Remember that oxygen is carried in the red blood cells and carbon dioxide is carried in the plasma.

 b) diffusion [1]; concentration/diffusion [1]; respiration [1]
 c) Many alveoli have a large surface area [1]; the walls of the alveoli are very thin / are only one cell thick [1]; there is a short distance between the air and the blood / the capillaries are close to the alveoli [1].
6. a) 25% [1]
 b) 70 [1]
 c) **Any three from:** increased risk of asthma; damage to cilia / cilia do not work correctly; lung cancer; bronchitis; damage to alveoli from persistent cough [3]
 d) The study only looked at two people / sample size too small [1]; only men were studied [1].

Working Scientifically
1. a) i) **Any one from:** wear goggles; hold the test tube in a clamp; do not point the tube at anybody [1]
 ii) They aways put 20 cm³ of water in the boiling tube. [1]

> Remember that in a fair test only one factor is varied.

 b) i) 24 [1]; 25 [1]
 ii) Pastry [1]; it has the largest temperature change [1].
 iii) They can then work out the energy in 1 g of each food [1]; they can make a better comparison of the energy [1].
2. a) add iodine solution [1]; look for a blue-black colour [1]
 b) **Any one from:** it is safer; to stop the liquid shooting out of the tube; to make the temperature even throughout the tube; easier to control temperature [1]
 c) i) The starch had been broken down/digested [1]; by amylase [1].
 ii) 40°C [1]
 iii) temperature [1]

Science in Use
1. a) i) They are very high in lipids. [1]
 ii) They contain good amounts of proteins. [1]
 iii) They contain good amounts of iron. [1]
 b) less transport of the nuts [1]; so less fuel is burned [1]
 c) **Any two from:** there are limited reserves of coal; coal is produced very slowly; trees can produce more nuts every year; carbon neutral [2]

Elements, Compounds and Reactions

Pages 28–38

Vocabulary Builder
1. a)

Key word	Definition
Oxidation	Using heat to break down a substance into simpler substances.
Electrolysis	Oxygen is added to a substance.
Thermal decomposition	When a fuel combines with oxygen.
Combustion	Using electricity to break down a substance into simpler substances.
Reduction	Oxygen is removed from a substance.

[4 marks if five or four correct; 3 marks if three correct; 2 marks if two correct; 1 mark if one correct]
2. native [1]; compound [1]; Ores [1]; pure [1]; reduction [1]
3. a) methane and oxygen **(can accept in either order)** [1]
 b) carbon dioxide and water **(can accept in either order)** [1]
 c) methane [1]
 d) oxygen [1]
 e) methane, carbon dioxide and water **(can accept in any order)** [1]
 f) methane [1]

4.

Metal property   Definition

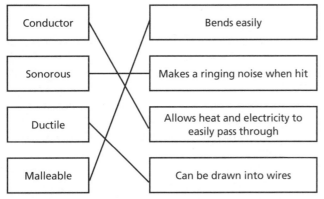

[3 marks if all correct; 2 marks if two correct; 1 mark if one correct]

Maths Skills

1.

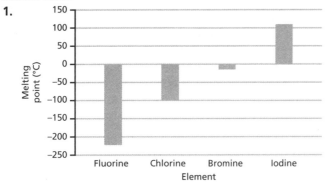

a) [1 mark for correct label on *x*-axis; 1 mark for correct label on *y*-axis; 1 mark for correct unit on *y*-axis]

b) Bromine   [1]

c) As you go down the group, the melting point increases.   [1]

2. a) Oxygen (**Accept** O or O_2)   [1]

    b) 25%   [1]

    c) Aluminium (**Accept** Al)   [1]

3. a) 0.58×1 [1] $= 0.58$ [1] kg [1] (Or: 0.58×1000 [1] $= 580$ [1] g [1])

    b) Not an ore [1] as the cost of the malachite (and the extraction) is greater than the money raised when the pure copper is sold [1].

Testing Understanding

1. a) **Accept two symbols from one group in either order:** Li and K; F and Cl   [1]

    b) **Accept two symbols only from one period in either order:** H and He; Li and C; Li and F; C and F; Mg and Al; Mg and Cl; Al and Cl; K and Ti; K and Fe; Ti and Fe   [1]

    c) Li **or** K   [1]

    d) F **or** Cl   [1]

    e) He   [1]

Make sure that you use the information on the excerpt of the periodic table rather than elements from your memory.

2.

Name	Formula	Number of elements present	Total number of atoms present
Water	H_2O [1]	2	3 [1]
Sulfur (di)oxide [1]	SO_2	2 [1]	3
Lead oxide [1]	PbO	2	2 [1]
Calcium chloride	$CaCl_2$ [1]	2 [1]	3

3. a) combustion (**Accept** burning or oxidation)   [1]

    b) ethanol + oxygen ⟶ water + carbon dioxide [1 mark for the correct reactants; 1 mark for the correct products; 1 mark for full equation using a '⟶' symbol (no mark gained if '=' used)]

When you write equations, make sure that the reactants are on the left of the arrow and the products are on the right. So, you write chemical equations like mathematical equations rather than on continuous lines like you would in English.

    c) Collect the gas [1] and mix with limewater [1]. It will go from colourless [1] to cloudy [1].

4. [1 mark for each correct cross, up to 6 marks]

Statement	Metals	Non-metals
On the left and centre of the periodic table	✓	
Solids at room temperature	✓	
Gases at room temperature		✓
Malleable	✓	
Oxides are acidic		✓
Oxides are basic	✓	

5. a) **Any one from:** (thermal) conductor; malleable; high melting point; unreactive with food   [1]

    b) **Any one from:** (electrical) conductor; ductile; high melting point   [1]

    c) **Any one from:** malleable; unreactive with water [1]

6. a) Oxidation (**Also accept** combustion)   [1]

    b) magnesium + oxygen ⟶ magnesium oxide [1 mark for the correct reactants; 1 mark for the correct product [1]; 1 mark for full equation using a '⟶' symbol (no mark gained if '=' used)]

    c) 3.9 g   [1]

Working Scientifically

1. a) The type of material.   [1]

    b) The lamp will come on.   [1]

    c) Hold the strip of material in crocodile clips.   [1]

    d) The material/components will become hot and could cause a skin burn.   [1]

    e) The lamp does not light up [1] because silicon is a semi-conductor [1]. (**Also accept** silicon does not conduct as well as a metal or graphite)

2. a) Conical flask (**Accept** 'flask') [1]
   b) Top pan balance (**Do not accept** 'scale') [1]
   c) Mass [1]
   d) Mass would appear to decrease [1] as a gas is made [1] and lost to the atmosphere [1].
3. a) They are too reactive [1] and would react with oxygen/water in the air [1].
   b) Wear eye protection/goggles [1] and gloves [1].
   c) The metals are less dense than water. [1]
   d) Purple/blue [1] because an alkali is formed [1].
4. a) He grouped the elements that behaved in a similar way in experiments. [1]
   b) He left gaps for elements yet to be discovered. [1]
   c) There are no gaps [1] and elements are listed in order of atomic number [1].
   (**Also accept:** additional group has been found; noble gases/group 0 are present)
5.
   1. Heat the lump of calcium carbonate strongly. [1]
   2. Allow the calcium carbonate to cool and put in a test tube. [1]
   3. Slowly add water until the test tube is nearly full. [1]
   4. Filter the mixture. [1]
   5. Collect the filtrate as this is limewater. [1]

   When you are writing a method, make sure that it is in chronological order.

Science in Use
1. a) Diamond [1]
   b) graphene [1]; diamond [1]
   c) C [1]
   d) 4 [1]
   e) 2 [1]
   f) 6 [1]
2. a) Sn [1]
   b) in the centre [1], with the transition metals [1]
   c) green [1]
   d) reduction [1]

Mixing, Dissolving and Separating

Pages 39–48

Vocabulary Builder
1. a)

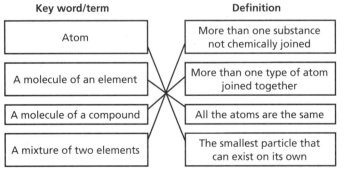

[3 marks if four or three correct; 2 marks if two correct; 1 mark if one correct]

b)

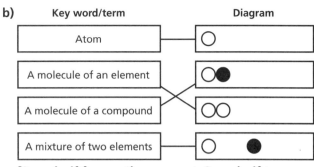

[3 marks if four or three correct; 2 marks if two correct; 1 mark if one correct]
2. solution [1]; Pure [1]; solvent [1]; solute [1]
3. a) Filtering [1]
   b) (Conical) flask [1]
   c) (Filter) funnel [1]
4. Meniscus [1]
5. a) Chromatography [1]
   b) Chromatogram [1]
   c) Retardation factor [1]

Maths Skills
1. a) 7 cm [1]
   b) $R_f = 3 \div 7 = 0.428571429$ [1]; 0.43 [1]
   c) ($R_f \times$ distance moved by solvent = distance moved by dye) = 0.85×7 [1] = 5.95 [1]
   d) 0 (**Also accept** the spot doesn't move) [1]
2. a) 78.08% [1]
   b) $\frac{1}{5}$ [1]
   c) 4 : 1 [1]
   d) 2 [1]
   e) 2 [1]
3. a) glucose [1]
   b) [1 mark for correctly labelled x-axis – sugar; 1 mark for correctly labelled y-axis – solubility; 1 mark for including the unit – (g/100 g water); 1 mark for scales that mean that the plot is over half of the graph paper; 1 mark for accurate bars plotted]

Testing Understanding
1. a)

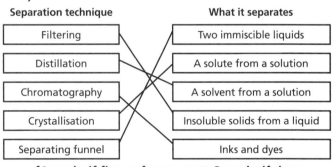

[4 marks if five or four correct; 3 marks if three correct; 2 marks if two correct; 1 mark if one correct]
   b) Filter [1], collect the filtrate [1], evaporate the water/crystallise. [1]
2. a) evaporation [1]; condensation [1]
   b) 100°C [1]

c) Pure **[1]** water **[1]**
d) Chromatography [1]
3. **a)** **i)** element **[1]**, compound **[1]**
   ii) element **[1]**, compound **[1]**
   iii) mixture [1]
   b) **i)** mixture [1]
   ii) compound [1]
   iii) element [1]

Working Scientifically
1. **a)** copper sulfate dissolved / a solution of copper
   sulfate was made [1]
   b) carbon/soot **[1]**; It's insoluble in water and so
   would form the residue **[1]**.
   c) copper sulfate crystals/solid [1]
   d) top pan balance (**Do not accept** scale) [1]
2. **a)** **Answers from the top in a clockwise direction:**
   thermometer **[1]**; (Liebig) condenser **[1]**;
   beaker **[1]**; Bunsen burner **[1]**.
   b) 100°C [1]
   c) To take the temperature of the vapour/gas **[1]**
   as it enters the condenser **[1]**.
3. **a)** A – paper **[1]**, B – solution **[1]**, C – solvent **[1]**
   b) So the pen doesn't run and make the
   chromatogram unreadable. [1]
   c) **i)** One dot moved vertically above the spot
   of the sample on the pencil line. [1]
   ii) More than one dot moved vertically above
   the spot of the sample on the pencil line. [1]
   iii) Only the one sample dot on the pencil line. [1]

Science in Use
1. **a)** filtration [1]
   b)

Fresh water
Filter paper in filter funnel
conical flask
Filtrate – water with insoluble particles removed

[1 mark for each correct label, up to 4 marks]
   c) **Any one from:** to prevent pathogens; to sterilise; to
   prevent water borne disease [1]
   d) **Any one from:** better teeth health; less tooth
   decay; fewer teeth fillings needed [1]
   e) Pure water only has water molecules in it **[1]**;
   drinking water is a solution and has other
   substances or named substances in it, e.g. chlorine
   and fluoride **[1]**
   f) distillation [1]

Forces and their Effects

Pages 49–59

Vocabulary Builder
1. air resistance **[1]**; lift force **[1]**; weight **[1]**

Air resistance is the force that air exerts on a moving object.

2. Rubber band [1]

A material is described as elastic if it returns to its original shape after being stretched/squashed/twisted/bent.

3. pulling **[1]**; compressive **[1]**
4. **a)** C [1]
   b) D [1]
   c) A [1]
   d) F [1]
5. **a)** newton-meter (**Accept** spring balance) [1]
   b) newton [1]
   c) N [1]
6. air resistance; friction [2]
7. **a)** True [1]
   b) False [1]
   c) True [1]
   d) True [1]
   e) False [1]
   f) True [1]
8. If the pulling force is doubled the stretch
   doubles. [1]

Maths Skills
1. **a)** 1 N [1]
   b) 5 N [1]
   c) It would damage the newton-meter or break/
   damage the spring [1]
2. **a)** increase = (35 – 20) = 15 cm [1]
   b) increase = (15 × 2) = 30 cm [1]
   c) length = (20 + 30) = 50 cm [1]
   d) elastic [1]
3. The container does not move. [1]

If the forces on a stationary object are balanced, the object won't move.

4. Increasing [1]
5. **a)** force = (2 × 10) = 20 N [1]
   b) force = (5 × 10) = 50 N [1]
   c) It is weaker on the Moon than on the Earth. [1]
6. **a)** speed = (50 ÷ 2) = 25 km/h [1]
   b) speed = (72 ÷ 3) = 24 km/h [1]
7. **a)** C [1]
   b) moment [1]

8. **a)** anticlockwise [1]
   b) C [1]

   The turning effect of a force is bigger the further it is from the fulcrum.

Testing Understanding

1. After being stretched / the force has been removed [1] the material returns to its original length [1].
2. She cannot use newton-meter C because it only reads up to 0.5 N or would be damaged [1]; The divisions on newton-meter B have a smaller value than newton-meter A [1]; so she should choose newton-meter B [1].
3. **a)** the spring [1]
   b) the Earth [1]
4. **a)** air resistance [1]; weight/gravity [1]
   b) The engine driving force is the largest [1] because it acts upwards and the other forces act downwards [1].
5. **a)** Measure the length of the spring [1]. Attach the weight to the spring [1]. Measure the new length of the spring [1]. Take the first length measurement from the second length measurement to get the stretch/extension [1].
   b) The spring is damaged [1]; weight doubles from 1 N to 2 N [1]; the stretch more than doubles or increases 3× [1]
6. Track length = 400 cm [1]; speed = 400 ÷ 20 [1]; speed = 20 cm/s [1]

   Change m to cm, and then use the equation: **speed = distance ÷ time**. Remember, there are 100 cm in 1 m.

7. motorbike [1]; because the car travels 50 km in 1 hour / because the motorbike travels further in 1 hour than both the car and the van [1]
8. diagram A [1]; there is a bigger distance to hinge [1] so smaller force needed to close the door [1].

Working Scientifically

1. **a)** 45; 70; 80; 20 [4]
   b) steel [1]
   c) Yes [1]; the mass needed to move the cube was reduced/friction much reduced [1].
   d) It is easy to make sure that the weight (or mass) of the cube was constant for all the materials tested [1].

Science in Use

1. **a)** total driving force = (2 × 350 000) = 700 000 N [1]
   b) 2 700 000 N [1]

   To just lift an object off the ground requires a force equal in size to the object's weight.

   c) distance = (2 × 900) = 1800 km [1]
   d) weight – D; air resistance – C; engine driving force – A; lift – B [4]
   e) increase; constant; decrease; increase [4]

Energy Transfers and Sound

Pages 60–71

Vocabulary Builder

1. **a)** thermal [1]
   b) kinetic [1]
   c) chemical [1]
   d) chemical [1]; thermal [1]
   e) kinetic [1]; thermal [1]
   f) chemical [1]; kinetic [1]
2. **a)** Yes [1]
   b) No [1]
   c) No [1]
3. True; True; False [3]

   If you are moving at a steady speed, your store of kinetic energy does not change.

4. The elastic potential energy decreases [1]; kinetic energy increases [1].
5. work; kinetic; kinetic; gravitational potential [4]

   An object above the Earth's surface has gravitational potential energy.

6. **a)** The thermal energy store of the cup increases [1]. The thermal energy store of the tea decreases. [1]
   b) a temperature difference [1]
   c) conduction [1]
   d) It increases. [1]
7. **a)** petrol (**Accept** gasoline or autogas) [1]
   b) pollute [1]
   c) oil/gas/coal [1]; change [1]
8. **a)** vibration (**Accept** oscillation) [1]
   b) air [1]
   c) It makes the eardrum vibrate. [1]
   d) longitudinal [1]
9. **a)** diaphragm; molecules; frequency/pitch [3]
   b) hertz [1]
   c) Hz [1]

Maths Skills

1. **a)** **i)** work done = (5 × 20) = 100 J [1]
   ii) work done = (10 × 25) = 250 J [1]
   iii) work done = (50 × 0.8) = 40 J [1]
   iv) work done = (600 × 2) = 1200 J [1]
   b) chemical [1]; gravitational potential energy [1]
   c) **i)** work done = (8000 × 80) = 640 000 J [1]
   ii) 640 kJ [1]
   d) work done = (100 000 × 3000) = 300 000 000 J [1]; 300 000 kJ [1]
2. **a)** work done = (400 × 0.6) = 240 J [1]
   b) 0.2 m [1]
3. chemical energy = (800 × 45 000) = 36 000 000 J [1]
4. chemical energy = (2200 ÷ 100) = 22 kJ [1]; 22 000 J [1]

   Remember, multiply by 1000 to change kJ to J

5. 300 m/s [1]
6. 20 000 Hz [1]

Testing Understanding
1. a) Pushing a full trolley along the full length
of the aisle. [1]
b) chemical; thermal [2]
2. a) work done = (1000 × 0.5) = 500 J [1]
b) 125 N [1]
c) True, True, False [3]
3. Y [1]; Z [1]; Z [1]
4. a) A to B [1]
b) D [1]

> Total energy has the same value before and after a change.

c) B to C [1]
5. The gong is still vibrating [1]; a sound wave needs a medium [1]; sound gets quieter because less energy can be transferred from the container / there are fewer particles to transfer the pressure wave / energy [1].
6. speed = 1.55 ÷ 0.00453 [1]; 342 m/s [1]

> Remember, speed = distance ÷ time

Working Scientifically
1. a) Thickness of the insulator may be a variable/may affect the transfer of thermal energy [1] and so must be controlled/kept constant [1]. A gap of constant width is created by having an inner and outer beaker [1].
b) Use the measuring cylinder [1]; measuring cylinder has divisions of smaller size. (**Also accept** beaker does not have a 250 ml mark) [1]
c) i) 17; 15; 20 [3]
ii) 1. cotton wool, 2. polystyrene beads,
3. sawdust [3]
d) [2 marks for two points correctly plotted at 25, 54 and 30, 53 and 1 mark for a smoothly curved line drawn]
e) more slowly [1]

Science in Use
1. a) from 20 Hz [1] to 20 000 Hz [1]
b) sound with frequency above 20 000 Hz [1]
c) Yes [1]; they have frequencies above 20 000 Hz [1].

> Reminder: to change kHz to Hz multiply by 1000.

d) reflection [1]
e) Sound moves fastest through solids [1] and slowest through gas [1].